The Great Dane

The History, Breeding Principles and Present State of the Breed

by Frederick Becker

with an introduction by Jackson Chambers

This work contains material that was originally published in 1905.

This publication is within the Public Domain.

*This edition is reprinted for educational purposes
and in accordance with all applicable Federal Laws.*

Introduction Copyright 2017 by Jackson Chambers

Self Reliance Books

Get more historic titles on animal and stock breeding, gardening and old fashioned skills by visiting us at:

Introduction

I am pleased to present this reprinted edition of Frederick Becker's famous book "<u>The Great Dane</u>". The book was first published in 1905 and contains the very early history of this breed. Prior to its release, no other book was available on the Great Dane, nor was another written for many years after.

As with all reprinted books of this age that are intended to perfectly reproduce the original edition, considerable pains and effort had to be undertaken to correct fading and sometimes outright damage to existing proofs of this title. At times, this task is quite monumental, requiring an almost total "rebuilding" of some pages from digital proofs of multiple copies. Despite this, imperfections still sometimes exist in the final proof and may detract from the visual appearance of the text.

I hope you enjoy reading this book as much as I enjoyed re-publishing and making it available to fanciers again.

With Regards,

Jackson Chambers

INDEX OF ILLUSTRATIONS.

INDEX OF ILLUSTRATIONS—*Continued.*

INDEX.

INTRODUCTION.

"A single grain of solid fact is worth ten tons of theory."

ANY attempt to write an exclusively scientific work on a certain breed, its peculiarities, breeding principles, etc., must result in failure. By learning and adopting the theory of a science we become faithful slaves of its rules, and are not allowed to go our own way contradicting these rules without giving evidence that by virtue of a discovery we are entitled to do so. Even in the attempt to breed for the same type by following the same principles of breeding, two breeders might produce quite different results, because each individual dog has his own peculiarities, with a more or less pronounced power of transmission, and, on this, the results depend. Our aim should be to study thoroughly these peculiarities in the different strains of our breed, and learn how to make practical use of the knowledge thus obtained. And if we succeed in doing this, and can boast of having become learned breeders, we must not attribute this to science alone, but also to experience. Science is comparatively useless without experience, and all that I have learned from personal experience, and also from the experience of older breeders, I reproduce in this book, which is not written with a view to giving advice to our old fanciers, who mostly have a wider and far longer experience than myself, but for the benefit of those breeders who are novices, many of whom, refusing to admit this, go their own way, threatening to ruin what the cleverness and experience of our learned breeders has built up.

It is quite useless to breed a dog possessing qualities of appearance which cannot be made use of, and if we would try to do so, we should not succeed because, while mental quality produce eventually a certain peculiarity in appearance, certain qualities of appearance will never bring about a mental peculiarity; I mean to say, that we should never try to modulate the formation of a " Non-Sporting " dog at the expense of his particular points of beauty with the idea of making, for instance, out of a Great Dane something besides a companion, perhaps a dog fit to compete successfully in the Waterloo Cup. The fact is that the appropriation of a Great Dane as a faithful and affectionate companion was synonymous with the ennoblement of the appearance of this breed which was, in the good old time, a coarse-built hunting race, and this is the only reason for its wonderful change towards an unsurpassable elegance, noble appearance and affectionateness. The Great Dane breeder's aim, therefore, must be to produce specimens solely with a striking appearance and nothing else besides; he must, however, watch the mental development as well, especially in a puppy, in order to prevent in time any outburst of ferocity which, if existing in adult dogs, is solely due to the negligence or irrational method of education.

I must mention, in order to show that this breed is predisposed to become ferocious, that Great Danes are sometimes brought up abroad by fostering an innate tendency to ferocity to become reliable watchdogs, and when I saw last summer in Austria such a specimen, I saw plainly that this mental quality had had an enormous influence upon his appearance—he was a coarse, tall and obese looking specimen, although an offspring from the best known champion strain of Austria.

From this point of view the mode of education of a Great Dane is of great importance. Our Great Dane, with his inborn activity and sometimes dangerous temperament, must not have all the freedom he wants, but the freedom we are willing to give him—in other words, obedience is the chief thing in the education of a Great Dane. Fortunately the Dane is, as a rule, very sensible when punished, and he must learn in time to understand and obey if we reprove him without using the whip. And this we should aim at, viz., to get a Dane to obey promptly. This method of education is also essential for showing a Dane—many of us have been pleased when a whistle from outside made certain dogs standing in the ring like statues. This is what I call education, but not the throwing of toys, rubber balls, calling of all possible and impossible pet names to make a dog show himself, to get the right carriage of the ears, and so on. A whip can be used to make a Great Dane obey promptly without making him by any means less affectionate; on the contrary, they learn the better to understand their masters who, on the other hand, must never leave good behaviour unacknowledged. The natural effect of this method is that a Dane rationally educated always tries to please his master, while badly brought up specimens find just pleasure in what they should not do, and these sort grow worse and become sometimes a nuisance when full grown, instead of affectionate and obedient companions.

The show records give a wonderful illustration of the enormous advance our noble breed has made during the last decades. England took a fancy in this breed because she missed a tall, active and noble looking companion before the Great Dane was introduced into this country. Apart from a few old breeders who have given up dog breeding altogether there exists, I suppose, not a single deserter of the younger generation who has deserted this fancy to start breeding another race.. I think the majority will agree with me: Once bred a Great Dane and never another breed! The attraction which a Great Dane offers gains him every year many new friends, and if beginners only possess some patience and a genuine love for this breed, taking, furthermore, dog-breeding as an ideal sport in addition to its material usefulness, they should in time succeed in what they aim. Breeding champions is by no means the privilege or the monopoly of our noted fanciers; he who has started with such a prejudice had really better retire. We should look forward, of course, to breeding a champion dog a day, and we must be ambitious to play an equally leading rôle as our prominent fanciers do, and for this reason we should follow and keep to their ways of breeding a first-rate Great Dane, and must not believe that we can do so on our own. Always pleased if an inferior dog is beaten, patient under disappointment, and never over-rating one's own stock— these are the main factors in bringing about healthy and productive competition. Exhibitors should always bear in mind: as many judges, so many opinions—they should never throw stones at old, experienced judges if these gentlemen or ladies don't award their dogs one of the much-desired three figures: 1st, 2nd, 3rd, but instead one of the much-hated three letters: c., h.c., v.h.c.,—patience, courage, indulgence and keenness—*in hoc signum vinces*, Great Dane fancier!

FREDERICK BECKER.

October, 1905.

CHAPTER I.

—

HISTORY.

A Great Dane which is not a " Dane "—Age of the breed—Origin—The hunting Boarhound called " Hatzruede " - Ennoblement—Period of building up the present type—The first Special Club—The " Deutsche Dogge "—Naming of the breed in modern times—" Ulmer Dogge "— " Dogue d'Ulm "—" Grosse Dogge "—" Daenische Dogge "—Grand Danois "—" Great Dane "—" German Boarhound "—The " eternal " Great Dane—A thoroughbred breed—Much discussed relation with English breeds —Supposed crossing with Greyhounds—Actual crossing with Mastiffs —Crossing with Deerhounds - Continental influences —Two hard blows— Quarantine Act—Cropping rule—Consequence of the " cropping rule "— Transitive state to the uncropped era—Success of the advocates of the " longears "—" Honour to whom honour is due."

— — —

IN naming our handsome breed "GREAT DANE" we simply follow a tradition without regarding the fact that the addition of the name of the northern nation to the chief characteristic in the appearance of the breed is quite at

ERRATUM.

—

Page 8.—For "*in hoc signum vinces*" read "*in hoc signo vinces.*"

Great Dane, and these specimens — so it must be assumed in the absence of any other reliable proof or origin—are the ancestors of the breed. Also in the good old time this tall breed was either kept as a hobby or for the personal protection of its owners. The particular quality—courage combined with enormous strength and resolution—made a Dane at that time a useful animal for hunting boar and deer, and this is the reason why, in the time when gun-powder was not yet invented, the hunters named these dogs " Hatzrueden."

The present generation of fanciers will not, of course, hunt boars with Great Danes because they cannot, and have returned, therefore, eventually to the custom of the oldest times when this breed was kept as a personal companion ; under different treatment, brought about by the different use of this breed, it has undergone a remarkable change in its appearance, and special attention has been paid to a gradual removal of the coarseness in head, coat, tail and body, while massiveness and substance has been further cultivated in order to avoid a decrease in physical strength.

The ennoblement of the Great Dane by careful breeding for quality and points dates only twenty years back, and since then a rapid and enormous progress has been made. It is due to the efforts of our conservative breeders that we can speak already of a perfection in type and appearance. The splendid example which England has given to the canine world by the admirable development of the "Non-Sporting" dogs as well, has also encouraged Continental breeders, and I believe that the few German Great Dane breeders have been among the first sportsmen to undertake to protect the interest of a breed by forming—A.D. 1888—the first Special Club—the " Deutsche Doggen Club." and adopting the universal name "*Deutsche Dogge*" for this breed.

Arriving now at the point of the naming of this breed, fanciers, especially in this country, labour under an absolutely wrong idea. in their belief that the " Great Dane " is really of Danish origin.

The inhabitants of Wurttemberg (South Germany) are

nowadays as keenly interested in this breed as they were
many years ago, and they were the first who sent and ex-
ported their dogs all over the world. Of the places particularly known on account of their fine Great Danes like
Stuttgart, Doos, Ulm, it is especially the last-named
which had a great reputation, and this gave rise to the
naming of specimens bought from Ulm, " *Ulmer Doggen,*"
or the " *Dogue d'Ulm* " in France. From Wurttemberg the
breeding of " Doggen " was spreading all over the German
countries, and northern fanciers for a long time accepted
the name " *Grosse Dogge.*" Later on foreign breeders
took a fancy to these noble-looking dogs, and particularly
Danemark played for a short time a prominent rôle in buying
" Doggen " in North Germany, breeding then their stock on
different lines to the correct type, viz. more slender and
smaller in structure, and sending them as " *Grand Danois* "
over the world. Now it seems to me that the first specimens ever imported into England have come from Danemark, and that from these old times the name " *Great
Dane* " has been retained till to-day. In seeing and hearing
that the " Deutsche Doggen Club " has proved the origin
of the breed to be German, it has often been tried to alter
the name " Great Dane," but the name " *German Boarhound* " has never found any influential supporters. The
" Great Dane " has taken a firm hold and, under these
circumstances, I feel sure that even our grandchildren will
not hear and know of the breed other than as the "GREAT
DANE."

All the above details clearly prove that the " Great
Dane " is as thoroughbred as any other breed and all argu-
ments and stories are, therefore, baseless that the breed has
Greyhound or Mastiff blood in its veins. Perhaps the wish
is father to the thought—absurd opinions like these are
based very probably upon the similarity in colour of the

BRINDLE DOGS.

CHAMPION VICEROY OF REDGRAVE.

Born March 2nd, 1899. By Ch. Hanniball of Redgrave—Ch. Valentine of Redgrave.

Breeder : Mrs. H. L. HORSFALL.

The property of Mrs. H. L. HORSFALL, "Morningthorpe Manor," Long Stratton.

Viceroy is without any doubt the best representative of his breed ever seen in this country ; he is a stockgetter of unsurpassable quality, and has never been beaten on the bench. He possesses the enormous advantage to most of the other noted stud-dogs of the present time that he has given by virtue of his extraordinary quality many a strain the fundament of their present value. The fact that with a single exception only all the Champions of the younger generation, viz. ; Ch. Vanguard, Ch. Venesta, the recently departed Ch. Loris and Ch. Superba are sired by him, speaks for itself. In his appearance we see the wonderful combination of elegance with substance. A most typical head, good size, magnificent symmetry in the outlines of the body, heaps of muscles and bones make it even for a hypercritical observer impossible to find any fault with him. Born in March, 1899, he does not show yet such signs of age which could deprive him of anything of his ideal appearance, and I am sure that every genuine fancier wishes with me that his breeder might further succeed in keeping him in such pink of condition as shown in this season.

A statistic of the sired prize-winning stock brings Viceroy far ahead of any Great Dane living —as a matter of fact his progeny gains far over the half of the winnings at all the leading shows.

It is most interesting to study the development of the "Redgrave" strain, the perfection of which we have to see in Viceroy. "My whole Kennel is of entirely Continental blood. My Danes have not a single English ancestor, and to that I attribute the whole success of my Kennel. . . . . I admire the Continental Danes enormously and have always tried to breed up to them, and keep free from English blood. . . . " This was Mrs. Horsfall's answer ("Our Dogs," April 16th, 1904), when jealous and unsuccessful breeders dared to criticise the type of the "Redgrave" Danes.

I have compiled the full pedigree of Viceroy, which can be traced back to 1876, and it will be seen from it that both the grandsires of Viceroy are bred in Berlin, coming from the oldest strains existing.

(1)   CHAMPION VICEROY OF REDGRAVE.

PEDIGREE OF CHAMPION VICEROY OF REDGRAVE.

SIRE: CH. HANNIBAL OF REDGRAVE

- Hannibal (15)
  - Alo—Zobel
    - Caesar—Pietschker
      - Caesar
      - Zampa I. { Nero I. (i) / Else I.
    - Werra—Schmidt
      - Caesar—Stahlecker { Karo / Diana—Buchholz
      - Carmen { Victor—Hartenstein / Zampa I. { Nero I. / Else I. / Wotan
  - Juno—Luettich
    - Marko—Zapfe
      - Marko—Grossner { Apollo (2) / Flora—Schmidt { Zampa I. / Hector—Spratt
    - Flora—Anthauer
      - Flora—Zapfe { Malta—Buchholz / Lord / Flora
  - Melac von Friesland
    - Harras III. (6)
      - Hellas
        - Harras II. (3) { Nero / Fanny { Riego / Bella / Lord / Liza
        - Nora—Doos (4) { Harras I. / Bella III. { Casters Leo / Bella III.
  - Ch. Emma of Redgrave (late Emma II.)
    - Flora
      - Flora—Lengenfeld
        - Halfdan (5) { Harras II. { Nero / Fanny
        - Bella—Lengenfeld { Fromm's Lady / Casters Leo { Hertneck's Lord / Lord
      - Caesar Lord Bravo Minka
    - Bella
      - Blankenhorn's Moreau (7)
        - Harras I. Blankenhorn's Minka (8) { Lord / Liza / Moreau / Flora
        - Bella II.

DAM: CH. VALENTINE OF REDGRAVE

- Primas (13)
  - Victor II. (12)
    - Harun (10) Norma
      - Harras I. Nation (9) { Hertneck's Lord / Liza / Junkermann's Nero / Flora Bella
  - Nora—Leyh (11)
    - Prinz
    - Prinzess
- Ch. Bosco—Colonia (14)
- Ch. Emma of Redgrave (pedigree as above)
- Flora Ansbach

{ Nero I. / Else I. / Dr. Caster's Leo / Messter's Flora

{ Nero I. / Bella

{ Lord / Flora / Riego / Bella

{ Nero I. / Bella

(1.) D.D. St. B. No. 609.*—Born 1876. Breeder, Nill-Stuttgart. Has won 1 Berlin, 1876 : 1 Hanover, 1879 ; 2 Berlin, 1880 ; 1 Elberfeld, 1880 ; must be regarded as the oldest ancestor of the entire modern Great Dane generation.

(2.) D.D.S.B. No. 223.—Breeder, L. Meyhoefer, Berlin. Won 1 Altenberg, 1886.

(3.) D.D.S.B. No. 32.—Born June, 1884. Breeder, Eisele-Stuttgart. Won 1 Brussels, 1887 ; 1 Hanover, 1887 ; 1 Stuttgart, 1887 ; 2 Cologne, 1889.

(4.) D.D.S.B. No. 196.—Born March, 1885. Breeder, B. Ulrich-Doos. Won 1 Munich, 1886 ; 1 Altenburg, 1886 ; 1 Brussels, 1887 ; 1 Hanover, 1887 ; 2 Stuttgart, 1887,

(5.) D.D.S.B. No. 238.—Born May, 1888. Breeder, Dr. Diesterweg-Wiesbaden. Won 1 Frankfort, 1891 ; 1 Munich, 1892 ; 3 Berlin, 1892.

(6.) D.D.S.B. 33.—Born October, 1891. Breeder, B. Ulrich-Doos.

(7.) D.D.S.B. 605.—Born 1885. Breeder, Blankenhorn-Stuttgart.

(8.) D.D.S.B. No. 175.—Born Feb. 21st, 1889. Breeder, Umhaeuser-Boeblingen. Won 1 Cannstadt, 1889.

(9.) D.D.S.B. No. 190.—Born June 18, 1885. Breeder, Junkermann-Stuttgart. Won 1 Altenburg, 1886.

10.) D.D.S.B. No. 40.—Born February, 1887. Breeder, B. Ulrich-Doos.

(11.) D.D.S.B. No. 198.—Born May, 1890. Breeder, I. Merl-Burglengenfeld. Won 1 Augsburg, 1891.

(12.) D.D.S.B. No. 113.—Born March 6, 1889. Breeder, J. Kugler-Stuttgart.

(13.) D.D.S.B. No. 86.—Born 1892. Breeder, A. Hohmann-Fulda. Won 1 Munich, 1894.

(14.) D.D.S.B. No. 766.—Born July 21st, 1894. Breeder, H. Koenlein. Won 1 Amsterdam, 1895 ; 1 Heidelberg, 1896 ; 1 Berlin, 1896 ; 1 Spa, 1896 ; 1 Munich, 1896 ; 2 London, 1897 : 1 Rotterdam, 1897 ; 1 Amsterdam, 1898 ; 1 S'Gravenhage, 1898 ; 1 Amsterdam, 1898 ; 1 Arnleim, 1898 ; 1 Rotterdam, 1899 ; 1 Rotterdam, 1900.

(15.) N.D.D.S. No. 1†.—Born December 28th, 1891. Breeder, C. Lüttich-Berlin. Won 1 Rotterdam, 1893 ; 1 Munich, 1893 ; 1 Arnheim, 1893 ; 1 London, 1893 ; 1 Amsterdam, 1894 ; 1 Dortmund, 1894 ; 1 Haarlem, 1894 ; 1 Antwerpen, 1894 ; 1 Rotterdam, 1894 ; 1 Cologne, 1894.

---

* D.D.S.B.=Deutsche Doggen Stamm Buch.
† N.D.D.S.=Nederlandsch Duitsche Doggen Stamboek.

three breeds and upon few other striking resemblances, but upon no breeding points whatsoever, although we have at present a few specimens resembling more a Mastiff or a Greyhound than a Great Dane. But these formations are due to accidents or wrong breeding and rearing principles, and must not be regarded in any way as proof of relationship with the two English breeds. And whoever studies the illustrations of a Dane of older times, will surely admit that these old specimens possessed far less resemblance or similarity to the two English breeds than sometimes modern specimens do, which makes me believe that crossings, especially with Greyhounds, have taken place in the last decade more than ever before. Crossing with Mastiffs has actually come to my knowledge, but this has not been undertaken from the point of view of "improving" the breed but in order to create quite a new strain—a ferocious-looking watchdog. The view of Continental experts that the Irish Wolfhound is a product of crossing of Great Danes with Deerhounds is emphatically opposed by old breeders of Irish Wolfhounds.*

Judging, however, from what we see nowadays there cannot arise the slightest doubt that the present show generation is as genuine and pure-bred as any Continental specimens, because our conservative breeders, in following willingly Continental advice, never gave the reins out of their hands, and careful judging, sometimes by Continental

---

* Both parties are entitled to their views. As a matter of fact the Irish Wolfhound, or better, a race bearing this name, is far the oldest big breed existing. The noted writer Strabo says, that the Irish Wolfhound has been imported into Gaul from the Pictes and Celts. Silius reports that this tall breed has been brought to Rome in order to take part in the fights in the arena between wild animals. About twenty years ago it was proved that the Irish Wolfhound was beaten in size by the German Boarhound, and both breeds were crossed with the consent of the Kennel Club. The product of this crossing is the modern Irish Wolfhound, but this makes no difference to the fact that the breed itself is one of the oldest extant, but has been improved by crossing with the Great Dane.

experts, separated in time chaff from wheat, showing novices which way to follow and which way to avoid.

No other breed in England has had to sustain such hard blows as the "Great Dane." Firstly, the introduction of the Quarantine Act forbidding the landing of dogs in this country unless detained for six months at a place supervised by a Veterinary Surgeon appointed or sanctioned by the Board of Agriculture, and secondly, the introduction of the law concerning the prevention of cruelty to animals forbidding the cropping of the ears of our Danes—have induced many old fanciers to give up breeding altogether.

Immediately after the Act against cropping came into force the breed lost a great deal of favour because the young long-eared specimens were handicapped when competing with the older cropped Danes. But this intermediate state was fortunately only of short duration—our old breeders did all they could to smooth the way for the uncropped Dane, and by nothing else than breeding "longears" of still better quality than their uncropped ancestors had, these fanciers have succeeded at last in bringing our handsome breed into the foreground of the present dog fancy, and I do not doubt that our younger generation of breeders will succeed in furthering our noble breed if they only keep in the ways shown and smoothed for them by such versed and true fanciers and judges as Mrs. H. L. Horsfall, Messrs. Leadbetter, Boyes, Schmidt, Fox, Nicholas, Gooby, Sparks. Everett, Herbert, Marples, Slack and others.

CHAPTER II.

BREEDING PRINCIPLES.

Art and technique of breeding—Personal taste and ideal—Breeders of
a wrong type—The eminent breeding quality of a Dane—Power of inheritance—Easiness of breeding good quality—Breeding for quality and not for
quantity—Prolific stockgetter v. Producer of quality—Stubbornness of
"quantity" breeders—Ill effects of quantitative breeding—Pecuniary
returns of litters—Quality v. quantity with a view to pecuniary gain—
The age at which to breed—Breeding from bitches at the first oestrum and
its consequences—Duration of the developing period—Breeding at the
second heat essential—Use of immature dogs for stud—Separation of
young dogs from bitches in season—Ill effect of premature exciting the
sexual instinct—Over-breeding—The advantage of breeding in the winter—
Superiority of winter puppies—In-breeding—The reason for in-breeding
some years ago—The luck of in-breeders—In-breeding now unnecessary—
Rational and compensative breeding—Warning against ill-advices.

EVERY breed possesses certain peculiarities, and a study
of these distinct qualities forms the basis of our
breeding technique, so to speak, upon which the breeders'
success depends. Like a sculptor working out the prominent characteristics of his "subject," our first duty should
be to study carefully and thoroughly the points of our breed,
and learn the art of breeding before we attempt this difficult
step practically with our favourite animals. Beside studying
the peculiarities and breeding points, we must also work out
our own ideal, and every breeder should, therefore, put the
question before himself and answer it: What is my ideal of
the Dane I intend to breed, and how do I propose doing so?
And he will not go for an untypical "ideal" if he cannot
give himself an explanation for the peculiarity of his own
individual taste; I mean to say, he would quickly change
his mind if he sees that his ideal of a Dane does not
correspond with the description of a typical Great Dane

given in the Standards of Points of our Clubs. There exist, as a fact, breeders who would like a Dane far more if he were built like a tall greyhound ; others fancy the mastiff body in a Dane, and these are just the people who should compare their "ideal" with the fixed type before starting breeding, and then it rests with them to decide between Great Dane, Mastiff, or Greyhound. Every attempt to breed a Great Dane on other lines than the fixed type or, in other words, to modify that type in any way, begets discord between fanciers, who can only succeed in what they aim by sticking to the correct type and boycotting all the mistaken persons who try to alter it.

The Great Dane has the enormous advantage over many other breeds in that, if bred to a particular type for some time, he has, thereby, acquired the power of transmitting his characteristics with a fair amount of certainty ; a fixed type even possesses the power of reappearing in the character of the second following generation, even if it has become somewhat effaced in the direct offspring. I am glad to state that all the points we are able to describe to-day as fixed and, therefore, inheritable, are characteristic and typical in every respect. I really do not know any unty- pical peculiarity in our noted strains which regularly appears in their produce, and how powerful the fixed correct type is can be seen from the fact that we can easily remove or improve coarse points in the head, short necks, long backs, etc., of inferior strains by virtue of the fixed type of superior families.

Bearing in mind this particular breeding quality of a Dane, we must say that novices who willingly follow advices given to them by old and experienced breeders can produce perfect specimens as easily as our oldest fanciers do, and it seems to me that this extraordinary quality of our breed forms the main attraction, and offers the principal reason

CHAMPION THOR OF REDGRAVE.

Born March 29th, 1901.   By Lord Topper—Ch. Valentine of Redgrave.
Breeder : Mrs. H. L. HORSFALL.

The property of Mrs. H. L. HORSFALL, " Morningthorpe Manor,"
Long Stratton.

Thor is a perfectly shaped huge dog with any amount of bones and muscles, sound and typical in head and expression, and a reliable stock-getter of first-rate and very tall progeny.   Sold to Mrs. Sparks in 1902, he was repurchased by Mrs. Horsfall about two years ago, and has sired since magnificent stock.   Far the best of his progeny is that lovely bitch Ch. Viola of Redgrave (out of Vrola of Redgrave) ; others are Star of India, Vendetta of Redgrave (out of Ch. Vanda of Redgrave.)

CHAMPION THOR OF REDGRAVE.

(2)

why the breed remains on the upgrade as opposed to a distinct decrease in the breeding of other hounds arising from a delicacy in their race or disagreement among their supporters as to the exact type.

The breeder's aim should be to produce Great Danes which will not only give personal satisfaction in regard to the pecuniary return, but also make his reputation as a producer of first-rate specimens. And for this reason we must breed for quality and not for quantity.

I know very well that prolificacy cannot be prevented in specimens predisposed to it, but in the majority of cases prolificacy is furthered by the reckless breeding principles of many fanciers. And in the cases in which prolificacy cannot be prevented, an attempt should be made to lessen it by mating the prolific specimen only once, and the numbers should be still further lessened by destroying all the weak-looking puppies in order to give the bitch a better chance of nursing the good ones.

A very bad custom, however, has arisen of drawing the attention of the public to the prolificacy of stud dogs and brood bitches instead of to their power of producing typical progeny. A prolific stockgetter of inferior puppies is as dangerous for the future of our breed as a stud dog siring few, but high-class progeny, is beneficial to it. The principle of supporting breeding for quantity is the bad point in the present state of the breed and, I am sorry to say, many fanciers turn a deaf ear to all the warnings and advices of experienced breeders, viz., to kill the weedy puppies which every big litter contains. Instead of doing so even the weakest and worst-coloured puppies are brought up, very often without the assistance of a foster-mother. Besides the harm they do to the reputation of such breeders these weedy specimens might become dangerous to the reputation of their sires and dams, and if these fanciers cannot understand at some future date a sudden boycotting of their stud dogs, or an antipathy to their produce, they must not put the blame upon anybody else but themselves.

As to the pecuniary return of a litter it is ridiculous to expect a better one out of 12 puppies of inferior quality than out of 6 superior ones.

The ideal side of our breeding must never suffer under the influence of the material side, and he who cannot afford to place the ideal side first had really better give up Danes altogether. He might find material satisfaction in breeding other dogs, the quality and future of which are not so dependent upon rational and ideal breeding principles as is the case in our fancy.

The age at which to breed is a most important item of breeding principles. Of the two factors in breeding, the bitch is, strictly speaking, the producer, and the dog the originator; I will take the weaker sex as the more important part first. The subject of breeding from immature bitches is widely discussed among different fanciers, but breeding from Great Dane bitches at their first season should generally be avoided, for this important reason, that a premature demand for fulfilling her sexual duty is synonymous with a cessation in her physical development, which is so essential in a Dane. A Great Dane bitch usually comes into use from seven to eleven months old, which means just during the time when our breed grows considerably. The growing process absorbs not only a great deal of the nourishment a bitch can assimilate, but also all the vitality she already possesses, and if we require our bitches to sacrifice, while in an immature state, their developing power for the benefit of their puppies, how can we expect of such specimens to become good show and reliable brood bitches, and how can we expect to get first-rate puppies from such immature producers?

From my own experience I am inclined to say that Great Danes of either sex cannot be regarded as fully grown before they are 14 months old, while the building up of their frames and the ossification of their bones—I mean to say, their growth into mature outlines—requires another 3-4 months. This is just the age of the second œstrum, and it is absolutely advisable, if not essential, to breed from a bitch at her second heat, because her bones are still slightly pliant; and a birth in the 16th or 18th month modifies her confirmation in a way beneficial to further litters. If, however, breeders omit to breed from bitches at their second heat—mostly the show "mammon" is responsible for this shortsighted principle—the bones become firmly set and the first whelping at an advanced age is, therefore, more risky; apart from the deplorable consequences of breeding for the first time from three-year-old bitches, which has often proved fatal in the extreme.

My above remarks as to the sacrificing of the power of development in an immature state refer, in a certain respect, also to dogs used for stud when not yet fully grown. The sexual instinct, being inborn, makes its appearance early in youngsters, but many fanciers refuse to understand why, in such cases, young dogs become bad doers when they are not separated from bitches in season. But as a fact they do, and mostly for this reason, and I even know cases where the omittance on the part of inexperienced breeders to separate dog puppies from bitches in season was the only reason why they remained bad doers for their whole life. On the other hand, a dog carefully considered in this respect, and kept away in time from bitches in season (in other words, not troubled during its developing period by sexual excitement) will seldom prove a failure in its first "*debût*" as a stud dog; if, however, it proves so, it must be regarded as an inherited or inborn fault. Premature

COUNT BRUCE.

Born July 22nd, 1902.   By Colonia Bosco—Countess Thelma.
Breeder, Mr. G. GOOBY.

The property of G. GOOBY, ESQ., " Roseneath," Whalley Road,
Manchester.

Count Bruce is a model dog with regard to substance and contexture of muscles, possesses very good size, is very active and a reliable stock-getter. Bruce is the most prominent winner of the Midland shows, having won numerous awards at leading exhibitions.

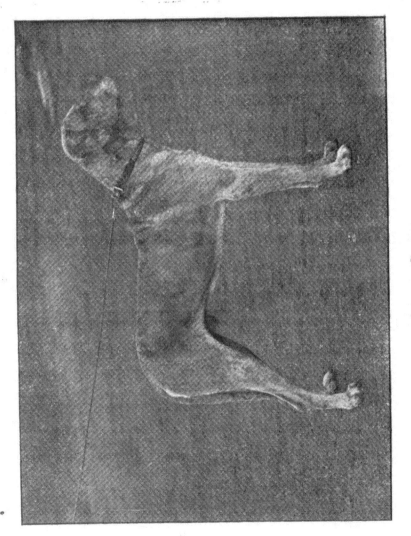

COUNT BRUCE.

(3)

exciting of the sexual instinct and the bad feeding connected with it is the chief reason for strong, big and active puppies becoming weak and lazy and growing only very slowly, apart from the probability of their becoming ferocious, especially if they see that all freedom is given in this respect to other dogs of the same kennel.

The over-use of stud dogs and over-breeding from brood bitches are fortunately no striking features of this breed in its present state. That we do not overwork our stud dogs is due to the fact that the majority of our breeders stick to their favourite colours, and as every variety has some reliable first-rate stock-getters the demand for the services of our noted stud dogs is well divided between them. As to our brood bitches—and I beg to remark that I only speak of noted specimens—their owners keep them as show specimens too, and this means that, at least, one of the two annual seasons is passed over.

I regard breeding from bitches coming in season from October to December as the most suitable and favourable opportunity for rearing healthy and strong puppies; or, in other words, I prefer winter puppies, in order to give them the chance of having warm weather for the time of the most important period of their development, and more than this, I regard warm weather as the best remedy against distemper, which disease attacks youngsters usually from five to seven months old. A bitch served, for instance, in November or December, comes in whelp between January and February; and, till March and April, winter puppies are protected against the cold by the substantial warmness which emanates from the bitch, while nursing her pups. Further, I have learned from my own experience that winter puppies possess more stamina and power of resistance to disease than summer puppies.

A very important item is the subject of in-breeding. In-breeding means the mating of animals more or less closely related to one another.   If we sometimes practise the principle of in-breeding (which in the human race often brings about the mental and physical collapse of a whole family), we must bear in mind that particularly in cases of " non-sporting " dogs we breed far more for prominent points of beauty in the appearance than for special mental quality, and from this point of view, and further, because the method of in-breeding involves the most reliable chance of getting a much-desired type, we venture to in-breed in order to establish a wanted type at the expense of the risk of eventually ruining mental quality.   The repeated in-breeding, which was the unavoidable consequence of the Quarantine Act, which prevented the introduction of fresh blood into this country, has, fortunately, done no harm whatever ; on the contrary, the in-breeders of the period from 1897 to 1901, when the whole future of our breed was seemingly dependent on a single strain, handled this business so carefully that their method has proved a gigantic success, and saved our breed from a threatening collapse.

In view of the steady improvement from generation to generation without any further in-breeding, this method must now be sharply condemned, especially since enterprising fanciers have succeeded in introducing fresh blood into this country just in time to replace our magnificent old stud dogs and brood bitches, some of which have gone this year to join their ancestors.

" Faulty points," and " lack of prominence in points," are two quite different things.   We must, therefore, distinguish between breeding for removal of obvious faults and breeding for the further improvement of existing points ; in other words, circumstances demand either rational or compensative mating.   My candid advice to novices is to leave compensative breeding to the old experienced breeders and to give all their attention to a rational method. As already said, the Great Dane possesses any amount of breeding quality. Young breeders must never try to remove prominent faults in their strains by mating their dogs with bitches having the opposite fault—for instance, the pairing of a dog having a narrow front with a bitch with a wide one. In Danes a correct formation is the best and most reliable compensator—a faulty bitch should, therefore, only be paired with a dog possessing the correct formation of the point in question and *vice versa*. If breeders would take the trouble to study the characteristics of the strains of the specimens to be mated in order to find out whether faults are inherited or not, and whether the parents on both sides have also been correctly formed in the point in question, it does not require special knowledge to select the right stamps of suitable breeding stock. Such a policy would keep inexperienced breeders from practising compensative mating which has already often spoiled the value of their good strains. I repeat—the Great Dane is, when himself full of inherited quality, a most reliable producer of quality—one might get, of course, from high-class breeding stock besides good progeny also a few inferior puppies, but, on the other hand, low-class parents will never produce a single puppy of quality. From this point of view the choice of dogs and bitches for breeding purposes carries the greatest weight with it, especially for novices, and this sort of fanciers must not trouble about getting a suitable breeding specimen for removing a fault by compensative mating, which means a choice of specimens seemingly fit to remove other defects by their faults, but must follow the way of rational breeding by pairing their faulty Danes with correctly formed specimens.

Compensative breeding for the further improvement of existing points is, however, essential on the part of breeders

Count Minshull.

Born May 25th, 1904. By Joubert—Countess Thelma.
Breeder: Mr. G. Gooby.

The property of G. Gooby, Esq., " Roseneath," Whalley Road,
Manchester.

This dog has certainly a great future before him; he proved a sensation when first time brought out at the Manchester Show, 1905. Minshull combines in his appearance the correct amount of substance with elegancy, has a very typical head, muscular body and sound limbs.

COUNT MINSHULL.

(4)

with a thorough and long experience, because a connoisseur must know by virtue of his observations which points can be improved by compensation and which can not, and it rests, therefore, with him to make all those improvements, which novices should not venture to interfere with. In saying this I mean that certain characteristics and points are rather hard to breed and, therefore, to improve, and the risk of a blunder should induce inexperienced breeders to listen to the more experienced and to consult them if they think that a particular mating of breeding stock might help, by compensative breeding, the improvement of existing points, but they must never venture to try compensative mating on their own initiative.

Finally, I must warn breeders against listening to any stories of a fancier with an " extraordinary" experience. For instance—certain breeders put the bitch to the dog when she is still discharging and, another time when the œstrum is nearly over, and they pretend to have observed that in the first case the puppies resembled far more the dam, and that the litter contained more bitches than dogs, and in the latter case that the progeny consisted of more dogs and were the very likeness of the sire. These are pure stories without any actual basis. We must never make a rule out of a coincidence. Those breeders inclined to share the above opinions, viz., that mating the bitch at the very end of the œstrum produces more dogs than bitches and so on, run the risk that even when the service has been effected apparently satisfactorily, the bitch will not prove in whelp at all. The most reliable moment for the service is the first day after the coloured discharge has disappeared.

CHAPTER III.

BREEDING POINTS.

The prominent breeding points –The head "mania"—Size –Inheritance of size—Breeding of size—Colour –Substance.

I REGARD height, colour and substance as the most important breeding points, and as the production of these standard qualities requires A1 breeding stock quality in head must come by itself. These three prominent qualities should be, as far as possible, combined to the exclusion of faults especially in the formation of the head—I mean to say, we should breed our Danes so perfect in these three points that by virtue of this perfection a somewhat faulty head would not handicap much. For years, however, the head was everything in our breed—deep, well blunted muzzles in specimens with a sometimes striking weakness of limbs have been and, in a few cases, are still preferred to inferior heads set on magnificent bodies. We should always bear in mind that our four-legged friends are nothing else than walking companions, and we cannot be pleased if a dog with a model head cannot walk a mile without getting tired out. We should not breed "sleeping beauties" but active specimens with a good amount of running power. A Great Dane must not be valued from the quality between the tip of the nose and the point of the occiput only, but all the other, and by no means less important characteristics, should be taken at least equally into consideration—a judging "by points" must arrive at a result as detailed above, viz., that perfection in body and general appearance counts far more than perfection in head only.

Of the points of general appearance, upon which I put the greatest weight, in the value of a Great Dane, size is the most essential contingent. Of all the breeds known in England the Great Dane is the only one in the name of which a special characteristic of the appearance is expressed, viz., size, and this point must, therefore, be regarded as the most important one we ought to breed for.

What do we call a tall Great Dane? The standard of points allows a minimum size of 30 inches to dogs and of 28 inches to bitches, but we must not be satisfied to produce specimens having these minimum heights—but should aim as much as possible at reaching the maximum, which I am inclined to put down at 35 inches for dogs and 32½ for bitches—in other words, we must breed and rear our Danes to get them within this margin. A dog standing 32½ inches at shoulder, measured with a foot rule, and not, as it is usually done, with a tape, and a bitch standing 30 are to be regarded as tall and fit to produce big puppies. They consider on the Continent that a few inches less do not handicap a harlequin, black or blue, in other words they regard brindles and fawns as the taller variety, but as I am not able to trace any reason for this conclusion, I am not inclined to make a rule of this Continental custom.

The question is widely discussed as to whether tallness is inherited, *i.e.* whether it is the prominent quality of a certain strain, or whether it is due to certain breeding principles. As to the inheritance of size, I think that there is an absolute possibility of breeding the desired specimens out of tall breeding stock. Also here we must observe that prolificacy is one of the principle reasons why we have so many undersized offsprings of big breeding stock. We see in so many cases small puppies sired by known giants which are, however, probably out of a litter of nine or more.

The natural method of breeding tall Great Danes is, of

MERLIN OF STAPLETON.

Born 30th April, 1902. By Ch. Viceroy of Redgrave– Lass of
Redgrave.

Breeder: Mrs. A. SPARKS.

The property of the Hon. W. B. WROTTESLEY, " Seisdon," Apsley
End, Hemel Hempstead.

This litter brother of Ch. Loris of Stapleton and Ch. Superba of
Stapleton is a perfectly coloured chestnut-brindle, of good size, typical
head, good expression, splendid body and legs, and a proved stockgetter.

Merlin of Stapleton.

(5)

course, to mate tall dogs with tall bitches and, if rationally and carefully reared, their progeny will reach a good size. We have doubtless—even taken proportionally—far less big brood bitches than tall stud dogs; I daresay there does not exist a single female standing, correctly measured, higher than 32 inches at shoulder and the majority are surely under 30 inches. On the other hand we have a fair number of very tall dogs and, judging from what I saw when last on the Continent, statistics regarding the size of home and Continental specimens would certainly show a result in favour of the former. And further, we can see that these tall dogs are mostly reliable stockgetters of big progeny even when mated to undersized bitches.

Inheritance of size is very prominent in certain strains, and furthermore, we are able to note many examples where a reversion to this quality in tall stud dogs can be seen in the size of the grandchildren although the latter are offsprings of undersized parents. From this point of view we can use average sized stud dogs from a noted tall strain with a fair chance of getting big puppies.

All these particulars apply, of course, also to brood bitches.

A tall offspring of an undersized family is absolutely the result of accident, and such exceptions must by no means be used as evidence in proof of the possibility of breeding big puppies out of an undersized strain.

In my advice on rearing Great Dane puppies I absolutely oppose the use of chemical preparations for furthering the growth in a Great Dane. In using such prescriptions, mostly advised by quacks, breeders must understand that they undertake such trials at the expense of the health of their dogs. The Great Dane grows and develops best on a natural diet; and all advice to the effect that excessive quantities of poisonous tonics assist and accelerate growth and development should be rejected as being extremely dangerous. Specimens with such ill-gotten gains never prosper, and especially from the breeding point of view, such poor creatures often prove valueless. I also know cases where the use of such drugs was the origin of a very untypical formation of the specimens so treated.

Next to breeding for quantity, breeders are nowadays very careless as to producing clean colours in a Great Dane ; our old fanciers have been far more conservative in this respect ; if they had not been, who knows what horrible markings we should have had to-day ? The only excuse, and that, I admit, a rather weighty one, could be given by breeders of harlequins, viz., that for want of a first-rate harlequin stock-getter they were always compelled to breed for chance, taking brindle or other coloured stud dogs. But nothing less than a crime against the fancy is the principle (carried out by a few younger breeders) of putting their well-bred brindle brood bitches to harlequin dogs ; and these fanciers are responsible for many horribly-marked specimens we so often see on the bench.

The **brindle** and **fawn** varieties are so far all right, but I recommend still more mating of brindles with fawns and *vice versa*, which method will greatly contribute to still more pronounced brindles ; I mean this will produce more sharply marked stripes, and also improve the golden ground in the fawns. **Blacks** have become, I am sorry to say, very seldom seen on the bench—it seems to me that this colour is not liked by the majority, although it is as typical as any other. The best blacks are to be obtained by mating clean-marked harlequins with black bitches ; also pairing blues with blacks produces jet-black stock. A mating of fawns with blacks, provided the latter are well bred, never produces good brindles, as I have read recently ; and they never do it in Germany, where a black bitch coming from brindle stock is regarded as badly bred. Of course, the mating of fawns with such badly bred blacks as are the offsprings of too densely marked brindle parents must result in getting brindles. Having only very few high class **blue** breeding stock, I recommend also mating blues and blacks, or blues and harlequins, in order to obtain blue offsprings.

Correctly and cleanly marked **harlequins** are to be obtained by mating bitches having much black ground to dogs with much white, or *vice versa*, in order to get a progeny with well divided black patches. But, as I have said before, there existed a deplorable lack of cleanly marked breeding stock, and harlequin breeders were, *nolens volens*, obliged to practice the worst breeding principles, viz., to breed for chances; I mean, they mated opposed colours, hoping that a lucky accident might deliver one specimen of the desired colour; but mostly, even this one did not arrive, and the fancy possessed a further lot of shockingly-marked specimens. Just the brindle-white Danes—their number increases—prove that the risk of inheritance of the opposed colours of sire and dam is particularly great in mating harlequin with brindles, and I know even cases where the colours of the offspring of the second generation, although sired by fairly marked specimens, has reverted to the paradoxical combination of colours of the grandparents. This means that, if this horrible colour is once inbred, it is nearly impossible to get it out again. A cleanly marked harlequin is the most difficult variety to breed, and requires, therefore, the purest marked breeding stock. I even know cases abroad where the mating of purest marked dogs and bitches, both coming from purest coloured parents, has produced bad colours, and as such risk is great we must pay the more attention to avoiding opposed colours. It should be borne in mind that there exist two related sides of the different varieties, viz., brindle and fawn on the one hand, and on the other, harlequins,

The Flamingo.

Born July 19th, 1901.   By Ch. Viceroy of Redgrave—Daisy of Letune.
Breeder : Mrs. KYNNERSLEY.

The property of Mrs. E. E. Fox, '' Littleworth,'' St. Helens,
Hastings.

Flamingo is doubtless the best brindle dog of the southern provinces,
a very tall specimen of slender structure with a beautiful stamp of head,
straightest legs and feet, good expression, well up in bones and muscles,
and with perfect ear and tail carriage.

THE FLAMINGO.

(6)

blacks and blues. Of these colours the former are the strongest, and if we mix the two different strains we get specimens where the brindle colour is the most prominent. We have plenty of them now, and their owners should not use these specimens for breeding harlequins, which are so difficult to get clear, but for producing brindles; the best way is to mate them with brindle bitches, and as the brindle variety is most easily bred, they might get by those wrong coloured stud dogs at least fairly marked brindles.

Article No. 1 in the Standard of Points of the GREAT DANE CLUB says:—"The Great Dane is not so heavy as the Mastiff, nor should he too nearly approach the Greyhound type," which is not quite right, as a Great Dane must not approach the Greyhound type at all. To put it clearly, the Dane should keep the golden middle between a Mastiff and a Greyhound. Also substance must be bred for, and that by mating only absolutely healthy stock, and also by avoiding any prolificacy. The most important point, however, for obtaining Danes with the correct amount of substance lies in the feeding and exercising principles, and my advice on the points is given to help breeders to get dogs of the correct weight.

CHAPTER IV.

REARING AND FEEDING.

When to begin with rearing—Additional food after the third week—
Feeding up to the eighth week—The age at which meat should be given—
Few hints—Dangerous and helpful drugs—Essentiality and effect of
feeding with meat—Feeding of bitches in whelp.

M ANY people believe that the rearing of a Great Dane
puppy starts after weaning. This is quite wrong; if
a sound and powerful bitch has only three or four puppies
to nurse, additional food after the third week is not so
essential as in the case of a bitch having double the number,
or more. A bitch has ten teats, but usually the front teats
and even the second row are non-functional, and in such
cases some of the pups must always wait till the others are
satisfied with food; a healthy pup is, however, seldom satisfied before it has emptied its place, and so it often happens
that some of the puppies will not develop so well as the
others, and then inexperienced breeders wonder why.
Everybody who has bred has surely observed how badly
stronger puppies treat their weaker brothers and sisters by
giving them no opportunity to obtain a full teat, and without additional food, we often notice when the time comes to
wean, especially a big litter, that at an age of 5–6 weeks
sometimes those puppies which were born the biggest have
remained behind the others. A rather general mistake is to
take the biggest puppies also for the strongest—I have
often observed that the tiniest of the whole lot never was
without its teat, pushing the others out of its way; these
smallest ones went on sometimes so well that after three
weeks I could not decide which were born small and which

stronger. The older the puppies become the more food, of course, they require, and in order to give the whole lot the same quantity or, at any rate, as much as they want, we must assist by giving additional food after the third week has gone.

For additional food to the nourishment of the bitch I recommend breeders, who can afford it, to give fresh cow's milk, which must have been boiled previously and cooled down to a lukewarm temperature, mixed with bread, Rodnim or Melox. If fresh milk is too expensive condensed milk should do, but I have noticed that this preparation does not conduce to ossification; puppies fed with tinned milk grow quickly fat, but the bones do not develop and harden quickly enough to carry the increasing weight, and the consequence often is that the front legs turn out at the pasterns, and the hind legs become somewhat cowhocked. This tinned milk will, however, have no ill-effects if it is given mixed with the " Plasmon " preparations, which are by no means drugs or tonics, but contain very substantial nutriments and regulate the digestive organs. " Plasmon " is for this reason most helpful, not only during the time of weaning the puppies, but also for the whole period of the development. As a change I would give the puppies from the fifth week gravy mixed with bread, Melox, Rodnim or rice. Furthermore, additional food must be given, because it facilitates the business of weaning the puppies, which is not so easily done as one might think, if the puppies have not gradually become accustomed to the change in the food; there should be no further change in this additional food before the puppies are eight weeks old, and already strong enough to be put on the meat.

Before giving advice on the further feeding, I must mention a few other important matters as to the treatment of puppies.

COLONEL BADEN.

Born March 2nd, 1901. By Soudan—Duchess.

Breeder : Mrs. REGINALD HERBERT.

The property of Mrs. REGINALD HERBERT, "Clytha Park,"
Abergavenny.

Colonel Baden is most probably the only representative of quality of
the older type. He is a cropped, beautifully marked brindle of enormous
size and substance, straight limbs, correct formation of back, and truest
Dane expression. Coming from the best family ever seen in this country
in earlier times, and representing the correct Continental type, he should
prove a valuable outcross to many a strain spoiled by wrong breeding
principles.

COLONEL BADEN.

⟨7⟩

Immediately after the puppies are born, one must look after dew-claws, and these are to be removed at once with a sharp pair of scissors; if this be omitted, and the pups allowed to grow up with them, they become cowhocked; if these claws are removed at an advanced age, it is often impossible to straighten the hocks again.

When the puppies are three weeks old the nails must be carefully cut, otherwise the scratching becomes too painful for the bitch, and makes her obstinate and bad tempered; she then shakes off the puppies.

From the sixth or seventh week the puppies should have their food and water dishes put on a stand, which must be just as high as the height of the puppies at the shoulder, and this stand must be gradually further raised according to the growth of the youngsters. If this be omitted the puppies can reach a dish standing on the ground less comfortably the more they grow, and the ill-effects of this negligence on the part of the breeders are: out-at-elbow formations, loose shoulders, and weak pasterns.

I take it that every puppy has worms, because a puppy free from this pest is a very rare occurrence, and almost not to be reckoned with, and if one happens to fortunately be so, a careful treatment together with the others cannot do any harm. Areca-nut, santonine, and all the other natural drugs, without any additional substance to weaken their poisonous character, are far too strong for puppies; I found "Ruby" very useful for a gradual but complete removal of the parasites in the intestines.

I have noticed mostly bad effects from giving chemical preparations, especially phosphates and so on, as tonics to puppies under five months. Useful as chemical food, for instance, might be for a dog at a more advanced age, a premature troubling of the delicate digestive organs of a puppy by giving preparations containing partly very poisonous substances, involves a risk without helping very much. On the other hand, Cod Liver Oil is a most magnificent tonic in every respect, and in cases where chemical matters are really needed for one or the other reason, we have, in Cod Liver Oil Emulsion, a suitable preparation. The argument that chemical food makes puppies grow more should be disregarded. It certainly makes substance and helps the ossification, but the bones, though they widen out, never grow. Novices must not believe the stories of people who have got a tall Dane by nothing else than natural growth, but who, not admitting this, boast that they have " made their dogs grow " by some secret means. This sounds very clever, but is nothing else than conceit, and we must laugh at it and not go begging such people to give away their precious secrets. A great Dane grows best unassisted, as everything does, in God's wide nature.

It rests, however, absolutely with the breeders to give their dogs all the chances of developing their inborn growing power by rational and careful feeding. A Great Dane, as any other breed, lives, grows and develops by the quality of food he can digest, not by the quantity of food he can eat. The food must, therefore, never be too bulky, and as dry as possible; the worst feeding principle is to stuff a young dog with sloppy meals which do not contain sufficient nutriments. As soon as the puppy has changed its teeth, feeding with milk, gravy, and other sloppy things must be stopped altogether.

I may draw attention to the fact that the best Danes, the ancestors of the present generation, were mostly brought up in slaughter-houses with butchers, and whoever goes, for instance, to Berlin will find the best specimens in the possession of wealthy butchers. I regard, therefore, plenty of meat the most important food for obtaining substance and strength. The Dane needs bone and muscle perhaps more than any other hound, and citing the aphorism: "Like begets like," meat remains the only natural producer of the desired substance in a Dane and should, therefore, be given as much as possible, together with some carbonaceous materials, viz., vegetables and boiled dog cakes. This should be the substantial meal to be given late in the afternoon, while in the morning a few dry biscuit cakes (Spratt's puppy or cod liver oil biscuits) will do. The second (midday) meal should consist of raw lean meat, starting with half a pound to be given to puppies, but not more than a pound should be given even to adult dogs.

A bitch in whelp requires a change in food. Only a little minced beef should be given, and plenty of sloppy food and much milk; and I recommend the addition of some lime to the water, which is very helpful for the development of the embryo. Regular weekly treatment for worms till the seventh week is essential, and diminishes the risk of having to treat later on fatal worm diseases in the puppies.

Regular brushing, treating for worms at least once a month, and, during the summer, a lukewarm bath every fortnight, are essential for keeping a Great Dane always in show condition.

LORD TOPPER.

Born February, 1895.   By Cæsar   Lehman's Floss.

Breeder : LEHMAN-BERLIN.

Late owner: Mr. H. SCHMIDT, 469, Hackney Road, London, N.E.

Lord Topper was one of the most popular dogs on the bench. Unfortunately a defect of the tail handicapped him severely, but still his show carrière was a very remarkable one, and also as a stud-dog he proved very successful. Having been very tall and heavy most of his progeny excel in size and substance. Far his best point, however, was his head with the genuine expression we meet so seldom nowadays. Topper was a very dark brindle. Mated with Ch. Valentine he sired Ch. Thor of Redgrave, doubtless the best of his progeny; other noted offsprings are Lord Methuen, Sir Victor, Baroness Topper, My Boy's Double and Leonore of St. Austell.

Lord Topper.

(8)

CHAPTER V.

EXERCISING.

EXERCISING methods often leave very much to be desired, and contribute a good deal to the lack of substance and activity in some specimens. Many fanciers believe it right to give a Dane just the same training as a working hound, and start, therefore, long walks with puppies of six months, or when even younger. Apart from the risk that through this the limbs may go wrong, for they are still too soft in a puppy even when seven months old, a young Dane is, as a rule, when healthy rather too active, and exhaustion is, therefore, the unavoidable consequence in a puppy which gets too long a walk every day. That a dog which is exhausted every day cannot fill out and gather flesh, does not need, I suppose, any comment. Before seven months old a puppy should not be taken out for a walk at all, but should be left in a kennel with a good yard, where it can run and jump about as much as it likes, and rest when it likes. The kennel must have a hard ground, which helps the much-desired formation of cat-paws. But even when grown up, excessive training is not to be recommended—gentle exercise, with short runs and some jumping, remains the best method to keep a Great Dane in good flesh, temper and condition.

Special attention must be paid to the exercising of bitches in whelp. The first few days after service exercise should not be given at all, and during the period of gestation one short, gentle walk a day will do, which should be continued up to the very end of the gestation as long as the bitch is willing to walk.

CHAPTER VI.

STANDARD OF POINTS.

THE GREAT DANE CLUB gives the following description of a typical Great Dane:—

General Appearance.—The Great Dane is not so heavy or massive as the Mastiff, nor should he too nearly approach the Greyhound type. Remarkable in size and very muscular, strongly though elegantly built; the head and neck should be carried high, and the tail in line with the back, or slightly upwards, but not curled over the hind quarters. Elegance of outline and grace of form are most essential to a Dane: size is absolutely necessary; but there must be that alertness of expression and briskness of movement without which the Dane character is lost. He should have a look of dash and daring, of being ready to go anywhere and do anything.

Temperament.—The Great Dane is good tempered, affectionate, and faithful to his master, not demonstrative with strangers; intelligent, courageous, and always alert. His value as a guard is unrivalled. He is easily controlled when well trained, but he may grow savage if confined too much, kept on chain or ill-treated.

Height.—The minimum height of an adult dog should be 30 inches; that of a bitch, 28 inches.

Weight.—The minimum weight of an adult dog should be 120 lbs.; that of a bitch, 100 lbs. The greater height and weight to be preferred, provided that quality and proportion are also combined.

Head.—Taken altogether the head should give the idea

of great length and strength of jaw. The muzzle, or fore-face, is broad, and the skull proportionately narrow, so that the whole head when viewed from above and in front has the appearance of equal breadth throughout.

Length of Head.—The entire length of head varies with the height of the dog, 13 in. from the tip of the nose to the back of the occiput is a good measurement for a dog of 32 in. at the shoulder. The length from the end of the nose to the point between the eyes should be about equal, or preferably of greater length than from this point to the back of the occiput.

Skull.—The skull should be flat rather than domed, and have a slight indention running up the centre, the occipital peak not prominent. There should be a decided rise or brow over the eyes, but no abrupt stop between them.

Face.—The face should be well chiselled and foreface long, of equal depth throughout, and well filled in below the eyes with no appearance of being pinched.

Muscles of the Cheek.—The muscles of the cheeks should be quite flat with no lumpiness or cheek bumps, the angle of the jaw-bone well defined.

Lips.—The lips should hang quite square in front, forming a right angle with the upper line of foreface.

Underline.—The underline of the head, viewed in profile, runs almost in a straight line from the corner of the lip to the corner of the jaw-bone, allowing for the fold of the lip, but with no loose skin to hang down.

Jaw.—The lower jaw should be about level, or at any rate not project more than the sixteenth of an inch.

Nose and Nostrils.—The bridge of the nose should be very wide, with a slight ridge where the cartilage joins the bone. (This is quite a characteristic of the breed.) The

Young Tyras de Grace.

Born April 13th, 1900.   By Tyras de Grace – Ch. Lore of Redgrave.

Breeder: Mr. R. Miller, Birmingham.

The property of Mr. J. Colles Carter, " Boyne View,"
Navan, Ireland.

This dog is certainly the best male offspring of the ideal Tyras de Grace, the fawn dog imported by Mr. H. W. Boyes.   He is 33 inches high, has about 40 inches chest measurement, possesses the most perfect outline of form and body and stands on the best of legs and feet.   His head is long and square to the end.   Being a member of one of the best families ever seen in this Country, he would certainly far more be used for the stud were it not for the long distance from the South of England and the Midlands.

YOUNG TYRAS DE GRACE.

(9)

nostrils should be large, wide and open, giving a blunt look to the nose. A butterfly or flesh coloured nose is not objected to in harlequins.

Ears.—The ears should be small, set high on the skull and carried slightly erect with the tips falling forward.

Neck.—Next to the head, the neck is one of the chief characteristics. It should be long, well arched, and quite clean and free from loose skin, held well up, snakelike in carriage, well set in the shoulders, and the junction of head and neck well defined.

Shoulders.—The shoulders should be muscular but not loaded, and well sloped back, with the elbows well under the body, so that when viewed in front, the dog does not stand too wide.

Fore-legs and Feet.—The fore-legs should be perfectly straight, with big flat bone. The feet large and round, the toes well arched and close, the nails strong and curved.

Body.—The body is very deep, with ribs well sprung and belly well drawn up.

Back and Loins.—The back and loins are strong, the latter slightly arched as in the Greyhound.

Hind-quarters.—The hind-quarters and thighs are extremely muscular, giving the idea of great strength and galloping power. The second thigh is long and well developed as in a Greyhound, and the hocks set low, turning neither out nor in.

Tail.—The tail is strong at the root and ends in a fine point, reaching to or just below the hocks. It should be carried, when the dog is in action, in a straight line level with the back, slightly curved towards the end, but should not curl over the back.

Coat.—The hair is short and dense, and sleek looking, and in no case should it incline to coarseness.

Gait or Action.—The gait should be lithe, springy, and free, the action high. The hocks should move very freely, and the head should he held well up.

Colour.—The colours are Brindle, Fawn, Blue, Black, and Harlequin. The harlequin should have jet black patches and spots on a pure white ground; grey patches are admissible but not desired; but fawn or brindle shades are objectionable.

THE NORTHERN GREAT DANE CLUB'S Standard of Points
is as follows :—

*The Chief Characteristics of a Great Dane are Great Size,
Immense Strength, and Activity.*

General Appearance. — An upstanding determined animal, with symmetrical outline of body, muscular quarters, head carried high on a long clean neck, standing strong and firm on all four legs, with proud alert expression.

The Head.—Should be long and well chiselled, with wide, deep and square muzzle, skull comparatively flat and rather narrow for size of dog, as little "bumpiness" in cheek muscles as possible compatible with strength. Stop not too pronounced.

Ears.—As small as possible, carried high and falling forward.

Eyes.—Expressive and alert, rounded in shape and dark as possible (Wall eyes in Harlequins not objected to).

Nose.—Should be dark or black (spotted or flesh coloured noses in Harlequins not objected to).

Neck.—Should be long and clean without loose or hanging skin (throatiness), carried high and with a slight arch, the junction to the head well defined.

Body.—Should have ribs well sprung, with belly well drawn up from a deep brisket, chest deep and well filled but not wide, not too long in couplings, a strong back with a slight arch and muscular loins.

Shoulders.—Should be well set and not loaded, elbows well under body.

Fore-legs.—Should be straight and strong, with flat bone.

Hind-quarters.—Should be strong and very muscular with well developed second thigh, well "curved stifles," and hocks well let down, which should neither turn in or out.

Feet.—Should be strong and well rounded and toes close.

Tail.—Strong at root tapering fine, and should reach to or just below the hocks, carried low, when the dog is in action or excited, it should be on a level with the back and slightly curved, but never curled over the back.

Coat.—Dense, short, and not soft in texture.

Action.—A free springy action with long swinging strides, indicating great galloping power, is very essential. Crampiness in shoulders or stiffness in hocks very objectionable.

Colours.—Brindles, Fawns, Blues, Blacks, and Harlequins (the latter should show clear black patches on a white ground) are preferred.

Height.—The minimum height of a dog, 30 inches; bitch, 28 inches.

Temperament.—The Great Dane is good tempered, highly intelligent, easily controlled, a perfect guard and companion. Being a dog of great activity it is very undesirable that he should be kept closely confined or on chain.

Faults most noticeable are:—Short head, weak muzzle, cramped or stiff action, curled tail, and coarse throat.

BRINDLE BITCHES.

CHAMPION VENDETTA.

Born August 21st, 1884.   By Harras—Flora.

Breeder: Mr. BAMBERGER.

Late owner: Mrs. REGINALD HERBERT, "Clytha Park,"
Abergavenny.

In saying that Ch. Vendetta was the true model of the older type, I wish to put her down as an example for comparison between the prominent points of beauty of the older type, and those many wrong points in the average Dane of to-day.   As I said in the respective chapter I regard size, substance and colour as the most important points we ought to breed for, and as the production of such standard specimens requires A1 breeding stock, quality in head must come by itself.   Looking at the illustration of Ch. Vendetta I cannot help thinking that such perfection all round has never been reached since by any Danes bred from English stock.   The ideal front, the rather short, but absolutely straight back, those heaps of bones and muscles, her extraordinary size of 32½ inches at shoulder, brilliant head - all these most desired points in a specimen of twenty years back prove clearly the correctness of my view, viz., that our younger breeders generation would far better succeed in producing first-rate animals by following the advices and sharing the views of our oldest breeders, instead of rejecting and opposing to the opinion of these experienced fanciers.

Champion Vendetta.

(10)

CHAPTER VII.

DEFECTS.

Head Lips—Neck—Throatiness of the Blue Variety—Stop—Cheeks and " Bumps " - Eyes—Ears—Length of Body—Symmetry.

PRACTICALLY speaking, everything is faulty in a Great Dane which does not correspond to the description of a typical specimen given in the Standard of Points. It is, therefore, useless to discuss such defects which every layman can see for himself by studying the standard and the appearance of his dogs.

But there are many details of formation in a Great Dane besides these obvious faults, and these are the subject of the following remarks.

The most striking defect in the head of many of our modern Danes is the want of substance in the foreface— " snipy " or " snouty " formations as we usually call this fault. This defect is of two kinds, some specimens looking snipy when viewed " full face," others snouty when " in profile." The origin of the former lies in the want of width in bridge of nose, and in the latter lack of lip-substance. Of course, a combination of the two is the worst. One animal, with fine square lips, can look snipy on account of the narrow bridge of its nose, while another, with sufficiency of nose width, can look snouty through want of lip-substance.

The nostrils, together with the front formation of the lips, should give the whole front of the head a blunt appearance ; but when the bridge is not wide enough, we see this fault very often, accompanied by the tip of the nose protruding, which gives the whole head, looking at it full face, a pointed appearance. I have observed, however, that the last named fault, which is mostly to be seen in youngsters, often disappears with age.

Some time back a discussion took place as to the natural and "artificially-made" lips, but, in my opinion, lips are, so to speak, born as everything else in a Great Dane. The fact that good lips are inherited does not allow any objec tions; if, on the other hand, lips are often "made," the progeny of breeding stock with artificial lips naturally cannot inherit this quality. In accordance with Article 10 of the Standard of Points the lips should hang quite square in front, forming a right angle with the upper line of the foreface. But squareness is far from being everything—a further and more important point, too, is the underline, in which so many specimens fail. This line must not only run straight from the corner of the lips to the corner of the jaw bone, but the line from the corner of the lips to the fold should be as much as possible parallel to the bridge of the nose, so that when a line is drawn from the root of the nose to the fold of the lips, we must obtain as nearly as possible an oblong.

But we so often see this shape :—

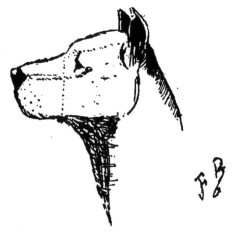

and that mostly in specimens with dewlaps, because the skin of the skull and upper part of the neck is not tight enough to pull the underline straight, and therefore allows it to run downwards, which causes the whole of the head to suffer in shape.

I recently discussed with old Continental breeders the peculiarity of Blue Danes being mostly throaty. The fact is that even the progeny of clean-necked breeding stock often turn throaty, and this makes my friends think that Blue Danes have a peculiar substance of skin, and as this skin itself is blue—a very light blue—it is not improbable that the skin of a Blue Dane, having a certain amount of pigment in it, is of a different quality to the colourless skin of the other varieties. The impossibility of breeding Blue Danes with clean necks induces Continental judges to disregard this faulty point in a blue specimen, but I do not share this opinion—dewlaps handicap a Blue Great Dane as much as all the other varieties.

Not only should the front part of the head form an oblong, but the shape of the head altogether. In order to obtain this oblong one has to draw the following lines : One from the tip of the nose to the point of the occiput, and another from the corner of the lips through the corner of the jaw-bone, as I have done in the following sketch :

What loose skin does in the underline is also done by a

Vrola of Redgrave.

Born February 20th, 1903. By Hercules--Ch. Valentine of Redgrave.

Breeder : Mrs. H. L. Horsfall.

The property of Mrs. H. L. Horsfall, "Morningthorpe Manor,"
Long Stratton.

Vrola is a superb golden brindle bitch teemed with quality all over.
She changed her owner several times, and this might be the reason that
when shown she was never in "Redgrave" condition. Judging from few
offsprings sired by Ch. Thor, especially the ideal Ch. Viola, Vrola possesses
obviously extraordinary breeding quality and should prove fit to fill out
the vacancy which Ch. Valentine left in the "Redgrave" kennel.

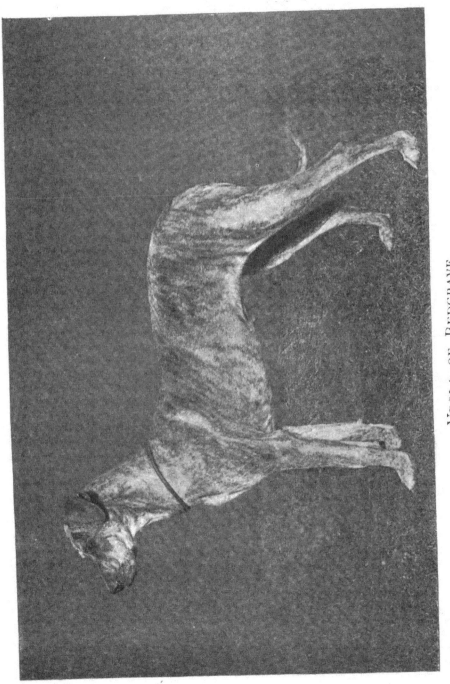

VROLA OF REDGRAVE.

wrong stop in the upper line. Besides the right stop, as given in the above sketch, we see faults in both extremes, viz., too much stop (dish face) or want of stop.

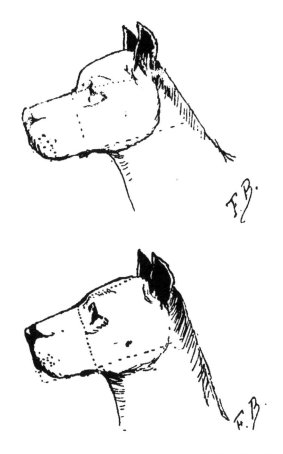

Want of stop makes the shape of the head suffer the most, for it gives the coarse appearance of an irregular oblong. Too much stop makes the forehead protrude unduly, and most of the specimens with this fault are pointer-like.

So much for the "profile" view. With regard to the "full face" appearance, the head should be laterally compressed, but by no means look like a "cigar box," which deprives the head of the true Dane expression. In this respect I prefer the description of the Northern Great Dane Club saying :" with as little bumpiness as possible "—to that of the Great Dane Club: "no lumpiness or cheek bones." I reject, of course, cheeky Danes, and more than this, I regard this as the worst fault in a head, giving it a clumsy and coarse appearance, but I maintain that a little bit of lumpiness contributes a great deal to a typical and sharp expression.

I miss, in the description of the Great Dane Club, any details as to a correct eye, and this is also a point which requires some improvement. The eye must not only be "expressive and alert, rounded in shape, and as dark as possible, etc." (as per the description of the Northern Great Dane Club), but first of all it must be small, with well developed eye-brows, which make the eyes appear deeply set, and contribute a great deal to a sharp expression. A defect often to be seen is a bright, full eye, a characteristic of a Greyhound, but very untypical in a Great Dane.

I think that the breeder himself is to blame for bad ear carriage, but not the dog. If the muscles of the ear are trained from the third month by very often calling the name of the puppy from a little distance, or by showing, for instance, to a puppy, a mouse in a trap, or something like that, we can all easily get the much desired Terrier instead of Greyhound ears in our Danes.

Gradually, breeders come to fancy a Great Dane with moderate length in the body. Too much length of body is as bad as too little—in other words, in this respect also, we must keep the golden middle. Of course the body, as a whole, should be rather long, but the point in length lies in the underline of the body, not in the outline of the back, which should be nothing more than moderately long, or, more correctly, shorter than the underline (chest line).

In order to show this point I give the accompanying two sketches, viz., of a wrong and a correct length of body:

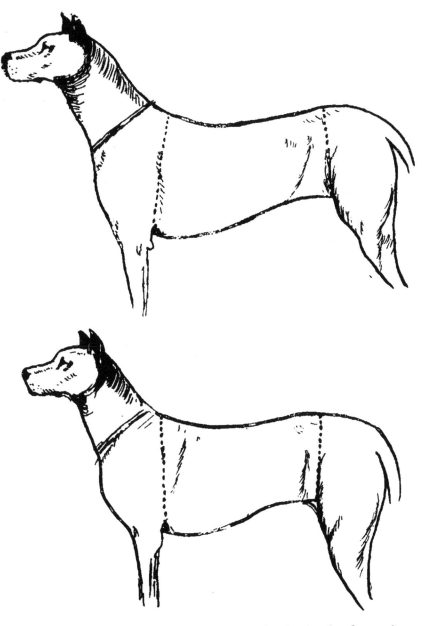

The fault of too long a back lies, firstly, in the formation of the shoulder and neck; secondly, in the formation of the

Champion Venesta of Redgrave.

Born September 29th, 1902.   By Ch. Viceroy of Redgrave—Libette
of Redgrave.

Breeder : Mrs. H. L. Horsfall.

The property of Mr. E. Bishop, 33, Osborne Road, Palmers Green, N.

Venesta must be regarded as the absolutely best Dane bitch in the Southern provinces.   She excels in all prominent points, viz., size, substance, colour, has an A1 head, wonderful neck and is built as straight as straight can be.

CHAMPION VENESTA OF REDGRAVE.

(12)

loin and hindquarters. Shoulders well sloped back and muscular, as they should be, shorten the line of the back, whereas, if loaded, they encroach upon the chest line. A long, well arched neck makes the back look shorter, whereas a short one makes the outline of the back appear too long. The slope of quarters should be as short as possible, and the thighs sharply arched on both sides, in order to shorten the outline of the back and lengthen the underline of the body.

The Great Dane is one of the most symmetrically built breeds. The important points in this symmetry may be seen from the following sketch, and I recommend breeders to make the same measurings of their dogs as I have done in this sketch, in order to see in which lines their specimens eventually fail :

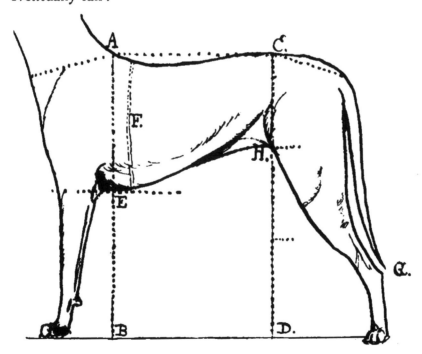

Assuming that a dog stands 30 inches at shoulder (line A—B), this should be divided into two parts of 15 inches each (point E), at the elbow and outline of the chest. Exactly the same result should be obtained if we measure the heighth of the hindquarters (line C—D), viz., 30 inches, but there are specimens either higher or lower at the hindquarters—the latter formation is called on the Continent the "hyena form." It is, however, usually more noticeable in puppies that the front and hindquarters are not of the same height, and this must not give rise to any disappointment before the dog is fully developed. In measuring the hindquarters, we see that from the crupper (Point C) to the angle of the hips (Point H) the distance is exactly one third of the whole height from the ground to the crupper. At a size in a dog of 30 inches at shoulder the circumference of the brisket (line F) must be at least 36 inches. The tail must just reach the hocks (Point G). A too long tail is to be regarded as a greater fault than a too short one.

CHAPTER VIII.

THE CLUBS AND THE PRESS.

UP to the formation of the Northern Great Dane Club the GREAT DANE CLUB was the only Association protecting and furthering the interests of our noble breed. It is, therefore, the oldest existing Club. There existed, however, an association of Great Dane Breeders many years ago, which was dissolved on account of the cropping, and on the ashes of the old Club the GREAT DANE CLUB was formed in 1895 at Cruft's Show.

No change has taken place in the leading office which Mr. Robert Leadbetter holds now in the tenth year. Vice-presidents are Messrs. H. L. Horsfall and A. Hood-Wright. The Club's delegate to the Kennel Club Council is Mr. Arthur Sparks, who fortunately has not often an opportunity of bringing up an important matter in protection of the interest of the breed, which clearly proves that the present state of affairs is very sound indeed.

Up to last year the office of Secretary was in the hands of Mr. Hood-Wright. Since February, 1904, Mr. Ernest Fox has been the Secretary, and it is noticeable that since then the number of members has risen from 70 to well over 100.

The Club possesses a valuable collection of Cups and Trophies :—

> The 40 Guinea Champion Cup for dogs.
> The 25 Guinea Champion Bowl for bitches.
> The 10 Guinea Junior Cup for dogs.
> The 10 Guinea Junior Cup for bitches.
> The 5 Guinea Cup for best brindle dog or bitch,
>   presented by Mrs. H. L. Horsfall.
> The 5 Guinea Cup for best fawn dog or bitch,
>   presented by H. E. Fowler, Esq,
> The 5 Guinea Cup for best harlequin dog or bitch,
>   presented by A. Sparks, Esq.
> The 5 Guinea Cup for best blue dog or bitch,
>   presented by F. Becker, Esq.
> The 5 Guinea Puppy Cup,
>   presented by Leonard J. Ching.

LORNA DOONE.

Born March 26th, 1904   By Jouber – Ch. Victory of Redgrave.

Breeder—Mr. CLIFFORD SLACK.

The property of Miss R. TOLLEMACHE.

This superb bitch has certainly a great future before her. She is of wonderfully golden brindle colour; other prominent points of beauty in her are an ideally chiselled head, long neck, perfect legs and feet; she is very roomy built and seems, therefore, to be a perfect brood bitch as well as a matter of fact she bred a splendid litter sired by Krishna.

LORNA DOONE.

(No. 13)

The Club supports many shows by guaranteeing good classifications, and offering their nice, newly struck Club Medals.

As to the classification, I hope that the Club will very soon return to a separation of the colours, viz., brindle-fawn and harlequin-black-blue, which proved a great attraction at the Kennel Club and Cruft's Shows in 1903.

The enormous increase in the breeding of Great Danes in the Midland and Northern provinces has given rise to the formation of a new Club, the NORTHERN GREAT DANE CLUB. Manchester is the domicile of many old breeders, and the Great Dane fanciers joined together in November, 1903, and formed this Club.

The President is Mr. W. H. Boyes, one of the oldest fanciers in the United Kingdom. The Vice-Presidents are Mr Peter Lawton and Mr. Clifford Slack.

The Secretary of this young Club is Mr. G. Gooby, an eminent director of Club matters, as the fact proves, that this young association has already over 60 members.

The property of the Northern Great Dane Club consists of :—

> The " Boyes " Silver Challenge Cup,
> The " Porthouse " Silver Challenge Cup,
> The " Taylor " Silver Challenge Cup,
> The " Slack " Silver Challenge Cup,

in addition to the Solid Silver and Bronze Medals, which are very nicely struck.

By guaranteeing classes, and offering Specials, the Club procures good classifications at leading Midland Shows.

Of the Press solely devoted to dogs, the interests of the Great Danes and their breeders are far the best catered for by the leading journal, *Our Dogs*. The detailed show reports written by experts or the judges themselves do justice to all exhibited specimens worth notice even it nothing be awarded them. Also the numerous correspondence dealing with Great Dane matters prove that partiality is a thing which the Editor of this valuable paper condemns absolutely.

Of other canine papers offering interest to Great Dane fanciers, I must mention the *Illustrated Kennel News*, *Stockkeeper*, the *Kennel Gazette*, (which contains the annual retrospects on the breed, and very often reports of judges), the *Shooting Times* (which should be read as often as Mr. Gresham is the appointed judge for our breed), and the short reports in *The Field*.

PREFIXES AND AFFIXES.

			KENNEL OF
Affix	REDGRAVE	...	Mrs. H. L. Horsfall
Prefix	SELWOOD	...	Mr. Hood Wright
Affix	STAPLETON	...	Mrs. A. Sparks
Affix	DE GRACE	...	Mr. W. H. Boyes
Affix	ESKDALE	...	Mr. Clifford Slack
Affix	ST. AUSTELL	...	Mrs. F. Becker
Prefix	CRESCENT	...	Mr. L. J. Ching
Affix	LOCKERBIE	...	Mrs. L. Fielder
Prefix	BEECHWOOD	...	Mr. Peter Lawton
Prefix	HIGHFIELD	...	Mr. G. Ray
Prefix	BITTERNE	...	Messrs. Tilling & Nicholas
Affix	ECCLESHALL	...	Mr. W. A. Walker
Affix	ROSEDALE	...	Miss E. Scott.

CHAMPION LADY TOPPER

Born August, 1894.   By Leo—Hilda.

Breeder : Mr. SCHOENBERG.

Late owner : Mr. H. SCHMIDT, 469, Hackney Road, London, S.E.

Ch. Lady Topper was a powerfully built specimen with a perfect head, straight back, nice thin tail, best of legs and feet and a brilliant mover.

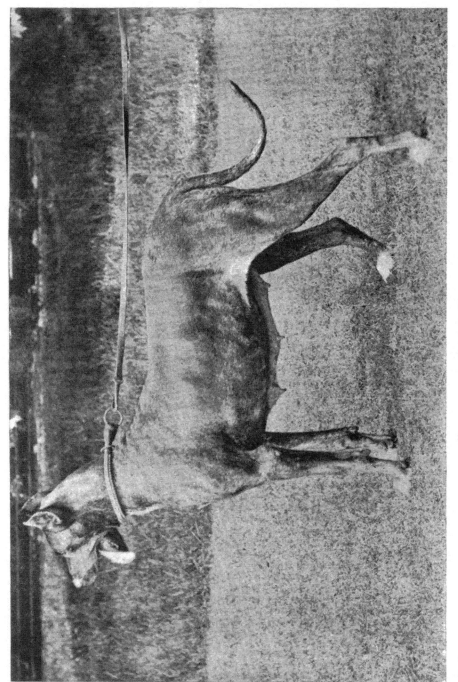

Champion Lady Topper.

(14)

FAWN DOGS.

CHAMPION VANGUARD OF REDGRAVE.

Born September 29th, 1902.   By Ch. Viceroy of Redgrave—Libett of
Redgrave.

Breeder : Mrs. H. L. HORSFALL.

The property of Mr. A. H. HALL, " West Croft," Lower Carley,
Near Reading.

Ch. Vanguard, the sensation of the K.C. show, 1903, is a magnificent
fawn with black shadings at the head, of extraordinary size, excels particularly in shape of the body, strong quarters and a nicely formed head.   He
is a winner of five championships, numerous first and special prizes, and
still holds his own as the best male fawn in this country.

Champion Vanguard of Redgrave.

(15)

COLONIA BOSCO.

Born February, 1895. By Hectar Peters—Minca.

Breeder : G. GERHARD, Berlin.

Late owner : Mrs. HORSFALL, "Morningthorpe Manor," Long Stratton.

This splendid animal was certainly the best male representative of the fawn variety ever seen in this country. He excelled particularly in shape of head, a blunt and very deep muzzle and a deeply set, rather small eye, which brought about a most typical appearance. A long, well arched neck, perfect front and limbs, and last not least, a correct line of back gave this dog an ideal appearance. His mating to Verona of Redgrave produced such fine animals like Silvia of Verona, Floradora and the recently departed Viscount. Another noted specimen by Colonia Bosco is Count Bruce (out of Countess Thelma.)

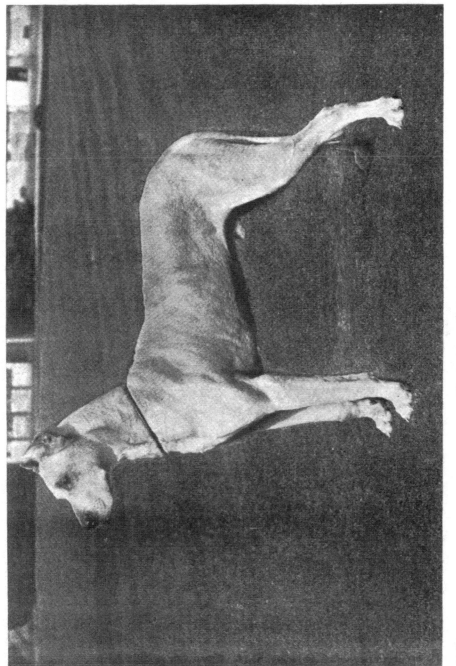

Colonia Bosco.

(16)

KRISHNA.

Born July 19th, 1901.   By Ch. Viceroy of Redgrave—Daisy of Letune.

Breeder : Mrs. KYNNERSLEY.

The property of Miss R. TOLLEMACHE.

Krishna is a specimen whose breeding value should be far more appreciated ; he is a huge fawn dog with a striking appearance, heaps of bones and muscles and soundest legs and feet. His show carriere shows great changeableness accordingly as to the different awards acknowledging his prominency in general appearance or neglecting this most important point.

KRISHNA.

TYRAS DE GRACE.

Born January, 1895.   By Tyras Rost—Maiblume.

Breeder : C. PETERS, Berlin.

Late owner : Mr. H. W. BOYES, " Summerfield," Manchester Road, Bolton.

Tyras de Grace was a light silver fawn, an extradordinary tall dog of lovely proportions all over.   He ran Ch. Hannibal of Redgrave very close for the best dog in the country at the first Hound Show at Ranleigh under the German Specialist Mr. Alberti, who reported, that with two such stud dogs as Hannibal and Tyras the breed should soon reach the height of perfection.

(18)   Tyras de Grace.

Count de Grace.

Born May, 1894.   By Rolf II.—Hera.

Breeder : G. Gerhard, Berlin.

Late owner : Mr. H. W. Boyes, " Summerfield," Manchester Road, Bolton.

Count de Grace was probably the largest Great Dane ever seen in this Country.   A lovely silver fawn, with a blue back, exceedingly long neck and perfect body.   The judges description of him first time exhibited says : An enormous brute of really awe inspiring proportion, but withal as elegant as a Great Dane should be.   A fine head, beautiful long, clean, graceful neck without a fold of looseness, smart shoulders, symmetrical body.   He died unfortunately very early, only about 4 years old. and only being in this country about 8 months.

COUNT DE GRACE.

(19)

CHAMPION COUNT FRITZ.

Born June 29th, 1890.   By Cyprus—Lorma.

Late owner : Mr. ROBERT LEADBETTER, Haslemere Park, Bucks.

This dog was a lovely fawn with a first-rate head, most typical expression, well arched powerful neck, perfect body, level back and exceptionally strong hindquarters.   He was the most prominent winner and one of the best stockgetters of his time—as a matter of fact Count Fritz was only beaten on one occasion.

CHAMPION COUNT FRITZ.

(20)

FAWN BITCHES.

CHAMPION EMMA OF REDGRAVE.

(Registered in Holland as Emma the Second).

Born March 16th, 1892.   By Melac von Friesland—Bella.

Breeder: Mr. FOPMA BONNEMA.

Late owner: Mrs. H. L. HORSFALL, " Morningthorpe Manor,"
Long Stratton.

Emma was imported by Mrs. Horsfall in 1896, together with Ch. Hannibal.   At the time of the purchase she was in whelp to the Dutch Ch. Bosco Colonia, belonging to Mr. Dobbelmann, and from this litter Mrs. Horsfall got Champion Valentine of Redgrave.   Emma was a superb bitch of extraordinary quality, especially in the head, which had a splendid front formation with the much desired blunt appearance, excellent lips, and that deep square muzzle, which has become one of the most prominent characteristics of the " Redgrave " strain.

CHAMPION EMMA OF REDGRAVE.

(21)

Champion Valentine of Redgrave.

Born February 6th, 1897. By the Dutch Ch. Bosco Colonia --
Ch. Emma of Redgrave.

Breeder: Mrs. H. L. Horsfall.

Late owner: Mrs. H. L. Horsfall, " Morningthorpe Manor,"
Long Stratton."

Champion Valentine combined in her appearance the different points of beauty of her noted parents. Valentine belonged to those very few specimens one would not like to see cropped : the type of the head was so perfect that it did not use the artificial ennoblement by shortening the ears. Her perfect ear carriage contributed, of course, a great deal to it.

Besides an unbroken record on the bench Valentine is the dam of numerous champions and prominent winners. Her mating with Ch. Hannibal produced the four champions —Viceroy, Victory, Viking, and Roger of Eccleshall. Mated to Lord Topper she produced Ch. Thor of Redgrave. Of other noted show specimens among her progeny I mention : Vesta and Verona of Redgrave (litter sisters to Ch. Roger of Eccleshall), Thelma of Redgrave (litter sister to Ch. Thor), Valina of Redgrave (sired by Tyras de Grace), Vrelst and Vrola of Redgrave (sired by Hercules, a dog imported by Mr. H. Schmidt and sold to Mrs. Horsfall), and many others.

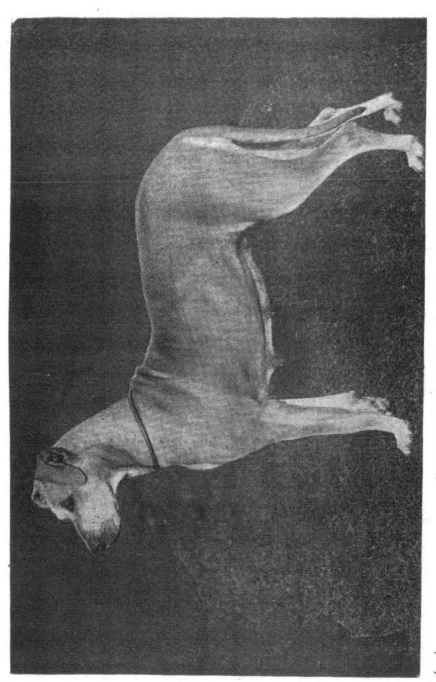

CHAMPION VALENTINE OF REDGRAVE,

(22)

LADY VOLCANO.

Born July 2nd, 1904.   By Joubert—Echo.

Breeder: Mrs. SALOMONS.

The property of Mrs. E. E. Fox, "Littleworth," St. Helens, Hastings.

Lady Volcano is a very typical fawn bitch, excellent body and shape, good bone and feet, and is straight all round; has a well formed head with a long foreface, square muzzle, and nice ears.

LADY VOLCANO.

(23)

HARLEQUIN DOGS.

FIGARO OF ST. AUSTELL.

(Registered in Germany as Brutus von Lichtenrade).

Born April 15th, 1903, By Thorwarth's Greif—Minerva von Culm.

Breeder: H. BRIX-LICHTENRADE.

The property of Mr. CLIFFORD SLACK, "Merryvale House," Nelson Road,
New Malden, Surrey.

Figaro was imported by me in March, 1905, and sold few months
afterwards to his present owner. He is a very tall harlequin with perfect
markings, has a most typical head — wonderfully chiselled, with a
strong broad muzzle — extraordinary long and absolutely clean neck, perfect
body and limbs, and any amount of bones and muscles. In style of action
he is superior to any specimen ever seen in this country. He is just that
specimen fit to save this variety from further crossing with opposed colours,
which was unavoidable up till now in the want of a pure-bred and sure
harlequin stock getter of quality. Being a cropped specimen he is not
allowed to compete in this country, but will certainly prove his quality as
one of the best dogs as sire of first-rate progeny.

FIGARO OF ST, AUSTELL.

(24)

CHAMPION LORIS OF STAPLETON.

Born April 30th, 1902.   By Viceroy of Redgrave—Lass of Redgrave.
Breeder : Mrs. A. SPARKS.

Late owner : Mrs. SPARKS, "Stapleton," Sawbridgeworth, Herts.

It is a sad coincidence indeed that the two champions of this best litter Mrs. Sparks ever had, viz.—Ch. Loris and Ch. Superba - both died within a few months.   A specimen fit to gain nowadays the most desired prefix must be perfect in all points, and so was Loris, who possessed extraordinary size, a head of truest continental type and expression, a massive and still elegant structure of body and sound limbs.   He was like his litter sister—Superba—a brilliant mover.   His show record was a most remarkable one, having beaten all dogs of the present generation, except Ch. Viceroy of Redgrave.

HARLEQUIN BITCHES.

CHAMPION SUPERBA OF STAPLETON.

Born April 30th, 1902.   By Ch. Viceroy of Redgrave—Lass of Redgrave.
Breeder : Mrs A. SPARKS.

Late owner : Mrs. A. SPARKS, "Stapleton," Sawbridgeworth, Berks.

The recent departure of this lovely bitch has left an irreparable vacancy in the "Stapleton" kennel.   There was really nothing in this specimen to find fault with —a model head ; perfection all over.   In addition to her standard appearance, an elegant style of action brought Superba for a long time far ahead of any specimen of either sex of this variety, and it goes without saying that her show carrière has been an almost unbroken record of winnings.

Champion Loris of Stapleton and Champion Superba of Stapleton

(25 & 26

Champion Senta Valeria II.

Born August, 1893. By Ciardi—Senta Valeria I.

Late owner: Mr. Robert Leadbetter, "Haslemere Park," Bucks.

With Senta Valeria the best continental Harlequin blood was introduced into this country. Having as sire that phenomenal old dog Ciardi, and as dam the ideal Senta Valeria No. 1, she was of course full of quality all over. A perfectly chiselled head with a strong and square foreface, very powerful neck, heaps of bones and muscles, and perfect legs and feet. The illustration having been taken in her last year does, therefore, not full justice to her. She was a great winner, was never beaten, and, as far as I know, left some magnificent youngsters in the "Haslemere" kennel.

Champion Senta Valeria II.

(27)

BLUE DOGS.

PRINCE BLUEBEARD OF ST. AUSTELL.

Born June 20th, 1902.   By Prince of Glencoe—Countess de Grace.
Breeder: Mr. H. SCHMIDT.

Late owners: Messrs. BECKER and SCHMIDT.

This dog was for a long time the only and a very typical representative of the blue variety—so much the more was his early departure a great loss for the blue fancy. Bluebeard was a dog of enormous size—as a matter of fact, the tallest specimen of his time—and had an exceptionally long head, good body, and fair legs and feet.

PRINCE BLUEBEARD of ST AUSTELL

(28)

BLUEBEARD OF ESKDALE.

(Registered in Germany as Champion Dojan the Second).

Born September 30, 1900.   By Dojan the First—Flora.

Breeder : A. RIXNER-LINZ.

The property of Mr. CLIFFORD SLACK, " Merryvale House," Nelson Road,
New Malden, Surrey.

Bluebeard has proved by his continental show record that he was not
only the best blue specimen abroad, but having beaten in Vienna, 1903, all
the noted German champions, he must be regarded as one of the best
Great Danes living.   He is not a tall dog, but the eminent quality of his
head, which is exceptionally long, laterally pressed, without any cheek
bones or bumps, his long absolutely clean neck, brilliant body, good tail,
and last, not least, his wonderful style of action, make of him one of the
best also in this country.   Having gained abroad the much desired
Champion Prefix, he can well renounce of winning prizes in England.
Being cropped he is not allowed to compete.   We shall see, most probably
within a year, that this ideal blue dog has given a firm fundament to the
future of this variety, which has nearly become extinct in the want of a
blue stockgetter of quality and sufficient first-rate brood bitches.

BLUEBEARD OF ESKDALE

(29)

BLUE BITCHES.

BLUE PANSY.

Born April 28th, 1902.   By Ch. Viking of Redgrave—Highfield Lady.

Breeder: Mr. G. RAY.

The property of F. H. FAWKES, 25, Upton Park, Slough.

This beautiful blue bitch is doubtless one of the best of this rare variety, having a superb head, perfect legs and feet, ideal front, and nicely short and dense coat. She does not fail in what the most specimens of this variety do, being absolutely clean in neck. Blue Pansy is a most reliable producer of Blue Danes, and, if mated to the right dog, is bound to produce first-rate progeny.

BLUE PANSY

Countess de Grace

Born March, 1897.   By Ingo- Cricket

Breeder: Mr. Gehrich.

Late owner: Mr. H. Schmidt, 469, Hackney Road, London, S.E.

Countess de Grace was in so far a remarkable specimen as she remained the only offspring from Ingo and Criket, the latter far the best blue bitch ever seen in this country. Countess inherited her parents wonderful blue colour and her dam's ideal head. A prominent winner in 1899-1900, she met then with an accident and was never shown again, but proved a perfect brood bitch of blue stock. The best specimen produced by her was doubtless Prince Bluebeard of St. Austell; mated in 1903 to Lord Topper she produced My Boy's Double and Leonore of St. Austell.

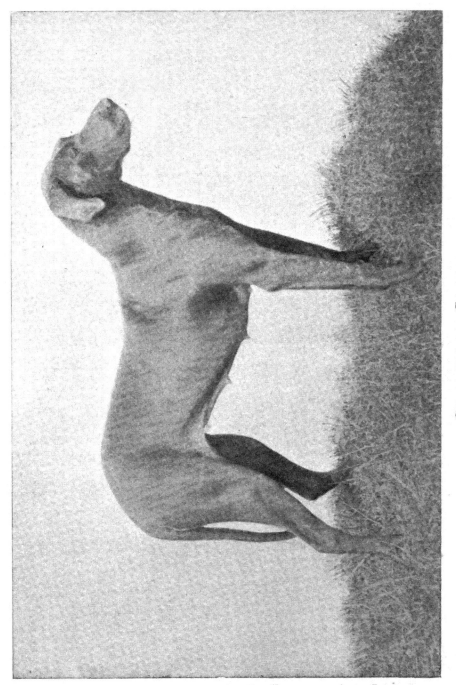

COUNTESS DE GRACE

BLACK DOGS.

SIR HECTOR OF OLDBURY.

Born June 7th, 1900. By Ch. Ronald of Redgrave—Bella of Redgrave.

Breeder : Mrs. H. L. HORSFALL.

The property of Mrs. E. E. MONEY-COUTTS, " Calcot Park,"
near Reading.

This specimen is certainly the best black dog in the United Kingdom
having a well-formed head with a blunt deep muzzle, a long nicely-arched
neck, perfect front and hindquarters, and a very nice shape of body. He
is only seldom shown, but was a prominent winner at Lanchester, 1904,
with Mr. Hood Wright as judge.

SIR HECTOR OF OLDBURY

(32)

BLACK BITCHES.

LEONORE OF ST. AUSTELL

Born August 8th, 1903.   By Lord Topper—Countess de Grace.

Breeder : Mr. H. SCHMIDT.

The property of Mr. CLIFFORD SLACK, "Merryvale," New Malden,
Surrey.

This bitch is most probably the best of her sex in the black variety ;
being tremendously boned, and having any amount of muscle, she is far
more predisposed to a brood than a show bitch. Her head is a study of
expression and type, and, combined with the correct substance in body,
this specimen shows the true continental type. She has never been shown,
but will certainly make her name as one of the best brood bitches in this
country.

LEONORE OF ST. AUSTELL

(33)

The German Great Dane Stud Book (D.D.S.B.) contains the following note about this dog :—" Nero the First should be regarded as the originator of the whole present Great Dane generation." As a matter of fact the pedigree of the " Redgrave " family contains Nero as the oldest traceable ancestor.

Nero the First.   1876

(34).

ROLF THE FIRST. 1881.

(Photo kindly lent by N. W. JACKSON, Esq., " Thornton House,"

Grosvenor Road, Birkdale).

The appearance of this dog, a son of Nero the First, a prominent winner at the Berlin Show in 1883, shows clearly how considerably our breed has improved since in quality of the head, whereas in properties of body, especially in straightness of back, contexture of muscles and amount of bones, the average dog of to-day is far inferior.

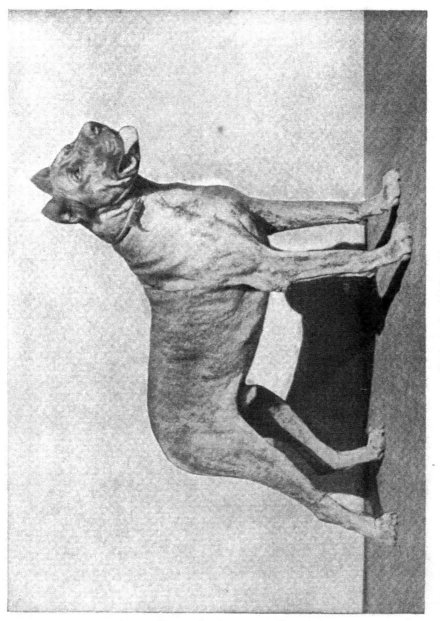

Rolf the First.

(35)

Made in the USA
Columbia, SC
14 October 2018